50

BASEBALL HALL OF FAMERS

Roberto Clemente

Robert Kingsbury

the rosen publishing group's
rosen
central

Published in 2003 by The Rosen Publishing Group, Inc.
29 East 21st Street, New York, NY 10010

First Edition

Library of Congress Cataloging-in-Publication Data

Kingsbury, Robert.
Roberto Clemente / by Robert Kingsbury. — 1st ed.
p. cm. — (Baseball Hall of Famers)
Includes bibliographical references and index.
Summary: Traces the personal life and baseball career of the Puerto Rican baseball superstar, from his childhood love of the game through his professional career and untimely death to his election to the Hall of Fame in 1973.
ISBN 0-8239-3602-3 (lib. bdg.)
1. Clemente, Roberto, 1934–1972—Juvenile literature. 2. Baseball players—Puerto Rico—Biography—Juvenile literature. [1. Clemente, Roberto, 1934–1972. 2. Baseball players. 3. Puerto Ricans—Biography.]
I. Title. II. Series.
GV865.C439 K56 2002
796.357'092—dc21

2001007917

Manufactured in the United States of America

Contents

Introduction

I f you had a Roberto Clemente baseball card from the 1960s or early 1970s, you would know many things about the Pirate right fielder. Bats right. Throws right. Height: 5' 10". Weight: 180 lbs. National League batting champion in 1961, 1964, 1965, and 1967. National League MVP in 1966.

Yet there was so much more to Roberto Clemente than the numbers on the back of his picture. Clemente broke into the major leagues at a time when few men of color, and even fewer Hispanics, played the game. He faced discrimination and racism throughout his career. He experienced insult and humiliation because of the color of his skin and the place where he was born.

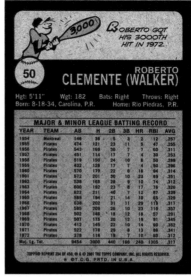

While baseball cards can give you many facts about an athlete, they rarely tell you what really made a player great.

The statistics on a baseball card don't give you a personal view. They don't tell you that the young man from Puerto Rico gradually won over the working class fans in Pittsburgh with his scrappy play and his love of the game.

Nor do they mention the battles he fought with sportswriters or the injuries he suffered. Baseball cards don't describe the moments of joy and triumph.

In this book you will see that Roberto Clemente was a real person. You will learn that he lived for baseball, but died for so much more.

Roberto Clemente, right fielder for the Pittsburgh Pirates, was an extraordinary athlete and a great humanitarian.

From Boyhood to the Big Leagues

Roberto Clemente Walker was born in the barrio San Antón in Carolina, Puerto Rico, on August 18, 1934. The fifth child of Luisa Walker and Melchor Clemente, Roberto had three brothers and a sister, who died tragically at age five when her dress caught fire. Roberto also had two half brothers and a half sister who lived in the Clemente home.

Life in 1930s Puerto Rico was difficult. Roberto's father worked on the sugarcane plantations, as did most of the men in the area. He earned forty-five cents a day when Roberto was a child. When he was promoted to foreman, his earnings increased to four dollars per week. In the United States, the average salary at the time was roughly five times higher. Though the Clementes always had

Roberto Clemente spent his childhood in the San Antón neighborhood of Carolina, Puerto Rico, not far from San Juan *(above)*, the island's capital city.

enough for food and clothing, there was little money for anything more.

When he was eight, Roberto asked his father for a bicycle, but even the used bike he wanted was too expensive. Melchor told his son that he would have to earn the money to pay for it himself. Roberto worked for a neighbor, earning a penny a day by taking a large milk can to the store, filling it, and bringing it back. When full, the milk can was very heavy. Roberto walked a long distance to and from the store. Roberto wanted the bike, so he stuck with the job even though at a penny a day, it would take three years. Three years later, the bike was his.

Roberto loved his parents and appreciated the sacrifices they made for him and his brothers and sisters. For example, during World War II, food in Puerto Rico was scarce. Luisa and Melchor insisted that their seven children eat before they did. Later, as a grown man, Roberto spoke often about the kindness and generosity of his parents.

Baseball Dreams

Little Roberto was wild about baseball, as were his neighborhood friends. They played all day and didn't care if they missed lunch. They played until it got so dark they couldn't see the ball anymore.

There wasn't much money for baseball equipment, though. So Roberto, his brothers, and their friends often made their own. They made bats from tree branches and from broomsticks. They made balls out of wadded up magazines and newspapers, or used rags, old

Stickball is a version of baseball played with a broom handle for a bat and a city street for a field. It is often referred to as the king of street games.

socks, and flattened cans. They made gloves and bases from old coffee bean bags.

Roberto loved to tell the story of a neighborhood game that began before noon one day and lasted until 6:30 that evening, when the boys were called for dinner. Roberto remembered hitting ten home runs that day.

There were times when Roberto's passion for baseball became too much for his mother. Luisa Walker wanted her son to grow up to be an engineer, not a professional baseball player. She wanted him to have the kind of job that would allow him to help people.

Over time, Luisa began to accept that her dreams for Roberto were different from those he had for himself. She saw how happy he was when he played baseball. That made her happy, too.

With every passing year, baseball became a bigger and bigger part of Roberto's life. When he wasn't playing, he often listened to Puerto Rican Winter League games on the radio. On Saturdays, his father would sometimes give him twenty-five cents—ten cents for the bus into San Juan and fifteen cents to get into Sixto Escobar Stadium. Roberto thrilled to see the players up close. Monte Irvin became his favorite player in the Winter League. A star of the Negro leagues, Irvin had a powerful swing and a strong throwing arm. In 1949, when Roberto was fifteen, Irvin crossed the color line to play in the major leagues. Two years before Irvin, Jackie Robinson had joined the Brooklyn Dodgers and become the first African American to play for a major league team.

During those Saturday afternoons, when Roberto was still a boy, he waited outside the stadium to see Monte Irvin and the other big leaguers arrive. For a long time, Roberto watched Irvin shyly. One day he mustered the courage to ask for an autograph. Soon the small, skinny boy from Puerto Rico was often seen following around the powerful outfielder from Alabama.

Roberto often carried his idol's glove into the stadium. Irvin sometimes gave the boy baseballs. Some children sleep with teddy bears; at bedtime, Roberto cuddled up with a baseball.

First Break

Thanks to Roberto Marín, Roberto's future took an exciting turn. A part-time high school teacher, Marín also coached a company-sponsored softball team. Marín watched Roberto play in the barrio with his friends. He was impressed with how they handled their guava-tree-branch bats and flattened-can balls. Marín saw something special in the lanky, fourteen-year-old Clemente. He asked Roberto to join the Sello Rojo rice company's slow-pitch softball team.

A Negro league star who played in the major leagues, Monte Irvin was a hero to the young Roberto Clemente. He is shown here at bat for the New York Giants in 1953.

Although Roberto had been playing baseball for years, this was the first time he played in an official league. Marín started him at shortstop, where Roberto was good with the glove and made spectacular throws from deep in the infield to first base.

When Roberto was sixteen, Marín moved his team to a fast-pitch league. He positioned Roberto in the outfield to make better use of his strong throwing arm.

During his high school years, Roberto joined the school's track and field team. His best events were the javelin throw, the high jump, the triple jump, and the 400-meter sprint. He once threw a javelin 195 feet. He leaped 6 feet in the high jump, and jumped 45 feet in the triple jump. With the 1952 Olympic Games less than two years away, there was some talk that Roberto might represent Puerto Rico in the javelin throw. Roberto knew that athletic glory in Puerto Rico was not won on the track or the field. It was won on the baseball diamond. And that's where Roberto wanted to be.

Roberto Clemente's talents were recognized by Dodgers' head coach Al Campanis during tryouts for the Santurce Crabbers of the Puerto Rican Winter League.

Through Roberto Marín, Pedro Zorrilla came to know the young Clemente. Zorrilla owned the Santurce Cangrejeros, or Crabbers, of the Puerto Rican Winter League. He also scouted for the Brooklyn Dodgers and other major league teams. He had a reputation for finding talented players and helping them reach the big leagues of American baseball.

Zorrilla and Al Campanis, the head scout for the Brooklyn Dodgers, held a tryout in Sixto Escobar Stadium. Seventy-two young players were invited, including the seventeen-year-old Clemente. Campanis had attended dozens of tryouts over the years. He rarely uncovered major league talent. This year would be different. During the first exercise of the day, Roberto threw a bullet from center field to home plate. Campanis couldn't believe his eyes.

Campanis asked Roberto to run the sixty-yard dash. He ran it in 6.4 seconds. Campanis was sure that there was something wrong with his stopwatch. After all, the world record at the time was 6.1 seconds. Campanis asked Roberto to run it once more. Again Clemente sprinted the distance in 6.4 seconds. Campanis realized that he had a genuine athlete in front of him. He sent all the other hopefuls home. The kid was good. Now he had to find out just how good.

Campanis needed to evaluate one other very important baseball skill: Roberto's hitting. When Clemente began to rip line drives into the outfield Campanis was impressed. Just as any good scout would, he watched Clemente carefully. He noticed that Roberto stood far back from the plate. He suggested to his pitcher that he throw some pitches over the outside part of the plate. He wanted to see how Roberto would handle them. Campanis watched as the boy continued to slap line drives into the outfield. To reach some of the outside pitches from where he was standing, Roberto often stretched awkwardly across the plate. This sometimes left him standing on one foot. Other times, he was left with both feet in the air! Campanis had never seen anything like this.

The Dodger scout was very interested in the young Clemente, but he couldn't offer him a major league contract because Clemente was under eighteen. But Clemente's talents were no longer a secret. It was only a matter of time until the big league clubs would come calling.

Contract Time

Pedro Zorrilla realized that his Santurce Crabbers could use a player like Roberto. The rules in the Puerto Rican Winter League did not prevent him from hiring the seventeen-year-old outfielder. Zorrilla offered Clemente a salary of $40 a week and a $400 signing bonus. Roberto wanted to accept the offer, but because of his age, he needed his father's consent. Not knowing what to do, Melchor Clemente asked a neighbor for advice. The neighbor suggested that Melchor negotiate for more money. So Roberto's father sent word back to Zorrilla that he should pay more for Roberto's talent. But Zorrilla wouldn't negotiate. Roberto sensed that his great opportunity was slipping away. He pleaded with his father to accept Zorrilla's offer. Finally, Melchor agreed to sign, and Roberto had his first professional contract. In the end, Roberto did receive something more in the deal: a much needed, new glove.

Batting Average

A player's batting average is calculated by dividing the number of hits by the number of at-bats. Walks do not count as at-bats. For example, a player comes to the plate four times in a game. He strikes out once, hits one double, flies out once, and walks once. He has gone one-for-three and has hit .333 in that game. A player who bats over .300 is considered successful.

Roberto played very little during his first year with the Crabbers. He was disappointed. The Crabbers already had a strong group of veteran players in the outfield. It was hard for Pedro Zorrilla to find opportunities to play an inexperienced teenager. Besides, Roberto had a reputation for swinging at every pitch. Roberto went to the plate only seventy-seven times that season, impressing no one with his .234 batting average.

Roberto was discouraged by his lack of playing time. He was also disappointed by his poor performance. He considered quitting many times that first season. James Buster Clarkson, a star of the Negro leagues and player-coach of the Crabbers, saw great potential in Roberto. He did everything he could to encourage him. Clarkson wanted Roberto to understand how bright his future looked. One day Clarkson told the young outfielder that he would be as good as Willie Mays some day.

Roberto played a lot more during his second season with the Crabbers. Some of the more experienced players weren't happy about losing playing time to the eighteen-year-old. But Clarkson felt that he had to put Roberto on the field. According to Clarkson, Clemente was "too good to keep out" of the lineup.

With increased playing time came greater success on the field. With greater success on the field came increased interest from major league scouts. Several teams closely followed Clemente's progress. In the National League, the Dodgers continued to show interest. So did the Milwaukee Braves, the New York Giants, and the St. Louis Cardinals. In the American League, the New York Yankees had also shown interest.

Realizing that there were several teams competing for Roberto's attention, the Dodgers wasted little time in making him an offer. They proposed a salary of $5,000 a year and a $10,000 signing bonus. This was the largest bonus they had offered a player since they had signed Jackie Robinson nine years earlier. Roberto knew of New York and he knew of the Dodgers. He didn't have to think twice. He wanted to play for them. He accepted the Dodgers' offer.

Not long afterward, the Milwaukee Braves made their play for Clemente, offering him a $27,500 signing bonus. Roberto was stunned. This was nearly three times the size of the bonus the Dodgers had offered. Unsure about what to do, Roberto confided in his parents. As soon as they heard that he had already said yes to the Dodgers' offer, Luisa and Melchor told their son that he must honor his commitment to the Dodgers. On February 19, 1954, Roberto signed a one-year contract with the Brooklyn Dodgers. The future of the young man from Puerto Rico looked very bright.

A Chilly Summer in Montreal

I n 1953, the Dodgers had one of the strongest starting outfield lineups in all of baseball. Jackie Robinson played nearly half the season in left field. He batted .329. Duke Snider played center field and hit .336, with 42 home runs and 126 RBIs. Carl Furillo played right field and had won the National League batting crown with a .344 average. Sandy Amoros, the Dodgers' top outfield prospect in 1953, led the International League in hitting with a .353 average. He looked to be a sure bet to get the call up from the minor leagues to the Dodger roster. The Dodgers did not appear to be looking to Clemente for immediate results.

Jackie Robinson, one of Clemente's contemporaries, was the first black player in major league baseball. He was inducted into the Baseball Hall of Fame in 1962.

Hiding Gold

Why, then, had they signed him? Were the Dodgers expecting Clemente to become part of the outfield in two or three years? Or had they signed him to keep other teams from getting him? There has been a great deal of talk and argument about this since the 1954 season. The Dodgers gave a hint about their reasons some years later. They seem to have drafted Roberto to keep him out of the hands of their arch rival, the New York Giants.

With no openings in the outfield, the Dodgers assigned Clemente to the Montreal Royals, their triple-A team in the International League. The Dodgers' management told Roberto that he would have a better chance to play in the minor leagues. They also told him he would gain valuable experience that would prepare him for the majors. What Roberto found was quite the opposite. He was not named the Royals' starting right fielder, and he did not play at all.

Roberto was confused by his coaches' responses to his play. When he played well, he was taken out of the lineup. When he played poorly, he was left in. During the first week of the regular season, Roberto hammered a ball over the left field wall and out of Delorimier Downs, the Royals' stadium. The ball traveled some 400 feet. It was the first time any player had hit a ball out of the park. To Roberto's dismay, he was benched the very next day. A few weeks later, he hit three triples in a single game only to find himself pulled from the lineup yet again for the next game.

What were the Dodgers up to? Were they bringing the young player along slowly? Many baseball professionals of the time have commented on the Dodgers' treatment of Roberto. Most believed that the Dodgers were trying to "hide" Clemente from other major league scouts. If other teams saw how good Roberto was, surely one of them would draft him.

A new rule had been established during the off-season. It required teams to keep newly signed players whose bonuses were $4,000 or greater on their major league rosters. If a team sent a bonus player to a minor league affiliate for any length of time, the player became available to all teams in the next season's draft. The rule had been written to stop the richer teams from hoarding all the young, talented players. Major league owners must have been unhappy with the rule. It was dropped before the start of the 1955 season.

The rule was in full effect during Roberto's season with the Montreal Royals, however. The Dodgers seemed to be trying to keep Roberto's talent secret from other teams. The Dodgers had him take batting practice with the pitchers.

This was very unusual. Max Macon, the Montreal Royals' manager, rarely put Clemente in the starting lineup. When Clemente did start, it was usually for the second game of a double-header, after most of the scouts had left.

The strange treatment by the Dodgers was bad enough. But there were other aspects of Roberto's situation that made life with the Royals difficult. Language was the first problem. Roberto had spoken Spanish all his life in Puerto Rico. He spoke only a little English. As a result, he felt isolated from many of his teammates and coaches. And in Montreal, most people spoke French. Fortunately, Roberto wasn't entirely alone. Chico Fernández, the Royals shortstop, spoke Spanish. Fernández became Roberto's roommate that season. Joe Black also befriended Clemente. Black was an African American pitcher who had learned some Spanish while playing baseball in Cuba and Venezuela.

There were the more serious matters of segregation and racism. Nine teams made up the International League in 1954. The other cities with teams in the league were Ottawa and Toronto

Racial segregation was still prevalent in the American South when Clemente began playing major league baseball for the Dodgers in the 1950s.

in Canada; Buffalo, Rochester, Syracuse, and Richmond, Virginia, in the United States; and Havana, Cuba. Richmond was part of the segregationist South in 1954. Whenever the team traveled there, Roberto and the other players of color had to stay in a separate hotel and eat in different restaurants from the white players. Roberto had lived his entire life on an island where nobody seemed to care much about skin color. To find himself suddenly the object of such inhuman treatment was very difficult for the nineteen-year-old from Puerto Rico. He resented it and was angered that many white teammates accepted it without question.

Second Chances

During those first months of his new life, Roberto was nearly overcome by his emotions. He was angry, frustrated, lonely, and homesick. And he was cold! Montreal is more than 2,000 miles from Puerto Rico—due north. Roberto had never experienced such freezing temperatures before. What the Canadians called spring felt like winter to Roberto.

It was thanks to Joe Black that Roberto got his next big break. Branch Rickey, the general manager of the Pittsburgh Pirates, asked Clyde Sukeforth, one of the team's coaches, to pay a visit to the Montreal Royals during a trip to Richmond. He wanted Sukeforth to see how well Black was pitching. The season before, Black had pitched for the Dodgers. He had been overused, though, and his pitching was now poor. The Dodgers had sent him back to the minors to find his "stuff" again. Rickey wanted to know if Black's pitching had returned to form.

At the time, the Pirates' team of 1954 had the worst record in the National League. They were on their way to finishing dead last. If they did finish in last place, the Pirates would have the first pick in the November draft. For this reason, they were eager to find a player who could help change their fortunes. A good pitcher could do just that for them.

Sukeforth arrived at the Royals' practice early one day to talk to Black. He asked him about the young pitcher who was taking batting practice and hitting so many balls over the fence.

Despite the Dodgers' efforts to keep Clemente a secret, he became General Manager Branch Rickey's *(above)* number-one draft pick for the Pirates in 1954.

Black told Sukeforth that the batter wasn't a pitcher at all. He was an outfielder, and his name was Clemente. Sukeforth learned shortly afterward that Roberto was a bonus player who had received more than $4,000. He would clearly be available in the November draft. Clemente saw no playing time while Sukeforth was in town, but the scout was able to watch Roberto take batting practice four days in a row. Sukeforth made note of Roberto's unusual batting technique. He also noticed that Clemente was able to hit to all fields. Before leaving Richmond, Sukeforth spoke to Royals manager Max Macon. He said, "Take good care of our boy." Sukeforth then sent word to Branch Rickey: "I haven't seen Joe Black, but I've seen your draft pick."

Rickey was thrilled with Sukeforth's discovery. But he wanted a second opinion. Used wisely, the first pick in the draft could make the difference between the road to recovery and continued failure for the Pittsburgh Pirates. Rickey sent Howie Haak, another top scout, to have a look at Roberto.

Unlike Sukeforth, Haak was able to see Clemente play in some actual games. In one of them, Roberto hit two triples and a double. He was replaced by a pinch-hitter late in the game. To Haak it was obvious that Macon was trying to hide Clemente. But the Royals manager had made his move too late. Haak had seen enough to know that Sukeforth was right. Roberto was their man.

As it turned out, it was lucky for both the Pirates and Clemente that Haak was in the stands the day of the three extra-base hits. Disgusted at being taken out when he was playing so well, Roberto stormed out of the stadium and returned to his hotel. He'd had it with Macon and the Royals. He was going home to Puerto Rico.

After the game, Haak went to look for Clemente. One of Roberto's teammates told the Pirates' scout that he thought Clemente had returned to the hotel with the intention of quitting the team. Haak went straight to Roberto's hotel. When he found the angry outfielder, Haak, who spoke no Spanish, did his best to explain to him what the Dodgers were doing and why. He also told him that the Pirates would use their first pick in the upcoming draft to select him. He would be their starting right fielder. He explained that if Roberto quit the Royals, the Dodgers would suspend him. That would make him ineligible for the draft. No team would be able to choose him. Haak asked Roberto to remain with the Royals and finish the season. It was for his own good and for the future good of the Pirates.

Roberto did not want to quit. He simply wanted a chance to prove himself on the field. Haak convinced him that the Pirates would give him that chance. And so, Roberto finished the season with the Royals and returned to Puerto Rico during the off-season. He played for the Santurce Crabbers once again in the Winter League. He played alongside one of the greatest players of the day: Willie Mays. Mays patrolled center field for the Crabbers that winter.

Branch Rickey flew to Puerto Rico at the start of the Winter League games to get a look at Clemente himself before the November 22 draft. During the first ten games of the season, Clemente and Mays battled each other for the league lead in hitting. Both were hitting over .400. If Rickey had had any doubts before his trip to Puerto Rico, they were gone now. Clemente was the real thing.

With Clemente and Mays in the outfield, the Santurce Crabbers were unstoppable that winter. They won the Puerto Rican Winter League championship. They went on to take the Caribbean World Series against the best teams from Cuba, Panama, and Venezuela. After the disappointing summer in Montreal, Roberto played with a joy he hadn't felt for a long time. It was good to be home.

Roberto Clemente would play in the major leagues for eighteen years, all with the Pittsburgh Pirates.

On November 22, 1954, during the first weeks of the Winter League season, the Pittsburgh Pirates drafted Roberto Clemente. They paid the Dodgers the $4,000 buy-out price for the rights to his contract. The Pirates knew they were getting a promising young player. What they didn't know was that within a few short years Clemente would come to be the heart and soul of the team.

From Last to First

Tragedy struck the Clemente family in the winter of 1954. Doctors discovered that Roberto's brother Luis had a brain tumor. Sadly, it was found too late for Luis to have any chance of survival. On December 31, just weeks after the cancer had been discovered, Luis Clemente died in a hospital in San Juan.

Throughout his brother's illness, Roberto went to see him at the hospital. One night in late December, Roberto drove home late. A drunk driver ran through a red light and crashed into his car. Clemente suffered a back injury that would plague him for the rest of his life. It would also prevent him from taking the field many times in his career.

Young Hero?

Roberto had joined the Dodgers when they didn't need him. The opposite was true in Pittsburgh in 1955. The Pirates had finished in last place in the National League the year before. What's more, they had not finished any better the two seasons before that. The Pirates needed help—a lot of it.

Each spring, the Pirates held training camp in Fort Myers, Florida, to get back in shape and see who would earn the starting roles for the regular season. Although Roberto was the Pirates' first pick in the draft, that didn't guarantee him a job as a starter. He would have to prove himself to the Pirate coaches.

An incident occurred during the first week of training camp that cast a cloud over Roberto. It also reminded him that some things had not changed since his season with the Montreal Royals. A local newspaper reported that a "Puerto Rican hotdog" had arrived in town. Roberto was shocked. The sportswriter had labeled him without ever seeing him play.

To Roberto, this was clearly another case of prejudice toward Hispanic players.

Roberto was angry and frustrated at being called a "hotdog." Fortunately, he did not allow himself to be distracted from playing baseball. In 43 at-bats that spring, Roberto had 17 hits for a dazzling .395 average.

Spring training doesn't last long, but the regular season does. It begins in April and lasts six months. Would Clemente be able to hit anywhere close to the same level over the course of an entire season? Probably not. The last player to do so was the great Ted Williams, who hit .406 in 1941. Nevertheless, the Pirate coaches didn't fail to notice that Roberto handled major league pitching just fine. He belonged in the majors.

The Pirates opened the season with three straight road losses. Roberto remained on the bench for all three games. Then, in the Pirates' home opener on April 17, manager Fred Haney made a change in the lineup for the first game of a double-header. Clemente would start in right field and bat third.

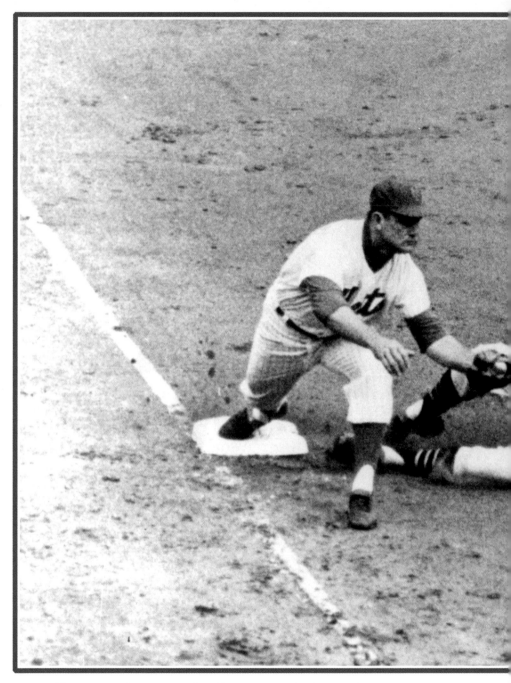

The aggressive base-running that Clemente showed in his very first major league at-bat continued his entire career.

In the bottom of the first inning, Roberto faced the Dodgers' pitcher Johnny Podres, who had just retired the first two hitters with little difficulty. Roberto pounced on one of Podres's first pitches and rapped a grounder to the hole between third base and shortstop. Pee Wee Reese, the Dodgers' shortstop, struggled to get a glove on the sharply hit ball and then fired a throw to first. Hustling down the first base line, Roberto beat Reese's throw and earned his first-base hit in the majors. Frank Thomas, the Pirates' clean-up hitter, followed with a triple to score Clemente. Unfortunately, Pirate heroics were few and far between that afternoon. The Dodgers went on to win the game 10–3.

Haney liked what he saw from Roberto in the first game, for he put Roberto into the lineup in the second game of the double-header. Managers often tinker with the roster early in the season. This time Clemente found himself in center field and batting first. Roberto played even better in the second game. He reached base twice on a single and a double. Once again, however, the Pirates could not muster enough offense to overcome the Dodgers. They lost 3–2. This was their fifth straight defeat since the start of the season.

Clemente's third start came at the New York Giants' Polo Grounds. Before the game, Roberto greeted Willie Mays, the Giants' center fielder. Monte Irvin, Roberto's boyhood idol, also played for the Giants that year. Roberto paid his respects to "Mr. Irvin," who suggested good-naturedly that Roberto call him Monte. During the game, Roberto added to the achievements of his first two starts with an inside-the-park home run. Once again, however, the Pirates were unable to win the game.

During the first weeks of the season, Roberto was hitting .367 and was ranked among the top ten hitters in the National League. Despite his solid play, the Pirates continued to lose. In fact, the team tied the National League record for most losses in a row to open a season. They won their first game after eight losses. The poor play that had kept the Pirates in last place three years running had not yet been repaired.

Although the Pirates won seven more games in 1955 than in 1954, they finished once again at the bottom of the league standings. After Roberto's hot start in April, his bat cooled off. By the season's end, his average had fallen to .255.

Learning the Game

Clemente's hitting suffered because pitchers learned that there was no such thing as a bad pitch to Roberto Clemente. If he could reach it, he would swing at it. He would also swing at pitches that were out of reach! As the season moved forward, pitchers served up fewer and fewer good pitches to Roberto. He began to strike out more often.

As the strikeouts became more frequent, Roberto's temper started to show. He took to throwing his batting helmet to the ground after a bad at-bat. Sometimes he threw the helmets so hard that they broke. Manager Fred Haney took Roberto aside one day. He let him know that he'd be getting a bill at the end of the season for all the helmets he broke. In all, Clemente shattered

One of Clemente's early challenges as a major league baseball player was to improve his batting technique.

twenty-two helmets that year. At $10 per helmet, that brought the bill to $220. Roberto learned his lesson. In future seasons, he found other, less expensive ways to express his anger.

Roberto learned to mistrust the press that first season in the major leagues. Reporters often quoted him phonetically. They exaggerated his poor English. An example can be found in a Les Biederman article in the *Pittsburgh Press* from June 1955. Roberto was quoted as saying: "Me like hot weather, veree hot. I no run fast cold weather. No get warm in cold. No get warm, no play gut." This kind of reporting was typical of the treatment Hispanic players received in the 1950s. While it is true that Roberto's English was not polished, many of his Pirate teammates from the 1950s have said that Clemente's English was just fine.

Roberto might have come to feel just as lonely and isolated as he had in Montreal had it not been for Phil Dorsey. Pirate teammate Bob Friend introduced the two early in Roberto's rookie season. Dorsey lived in Pittsburgh, and he immediately took Roberto under his wing. He looked after Clemente during his first months in the city. The two became good friends and remained that way for the rest of Roberto's life.

When Dorsey learned that Roberto didn't have a car, he offered to drive him to restaurants and other places. Dorsey also noticed the depressing, poorly maintained residential hotel where Roberto was living. The only thing that could be said in its favor was that it was close to Forbes Field, where the

Pirates played. Dorsey helped Roberto move into the home of Mr. and Mrs. Stanley Garland. Mr. Garland worked for the post office, and Mrs. Garland was a nurse. Roberto shared a room in their home with his teammate Roman Mejias.

If the press didn't take to Roberto in 1955, Pirates fans certainly did. And they had good reason. Roberto played the game with joy, intensity, and a touch of recklessness that touched fans. From his base running to his breathtaking throws from right field, Roberto gave the fans many exciting moments.

Roberto never forgot what it was like to be a fan. He often stayed behind for a few hours after home games to sign autographs and talk to fans. With his dashing good looks, he soon became a favorite among young female fans.

Bobby Bragan became the new Pittsburgh Pirates manager for the 1956 season. Bragan wasted little time in getting Gene Sisler to work on Roberto's poor batting technique. Sisler was a Hall of Famer and one of the Pirates' hitting coaches. The first order of business was to get

Despite some negative press in the beginning, Clemente soon became a favorite among Pirates fans, who admired his exciting play and charismatic personality.

Roberto to hold his head steady while swinging. Sisler was convinced that Roberto took his eye off the ball as he swung because of his head bobbing. Sisler had a second, bigger job on his hands: He needed to work on Roberto's batting eye. It was leading him to chase far too many bad pitches.

Roberto wanted to improve, so he listened carefully to Sisler. He worked hard on his technique. Little by little, the adjustments took hold. Roberto began to become a more reliable hitter. For a time in June he was hitting third in the National League with a .357 average. At the same time, the Pirates stood alone in first place. But neither the Pirates nor Clemente were ready to perform at this level for the length of an entire season. In the end, the Pirates finished in seventh place, second to last in the league. Roberto closed the season hitting .311. This was a huge improvement over his rookie season. Clemente collected 169 hits, hit 7 home runs, and drove in 60 runs. All in all, it was a solid performance. Roberto was beginning to feel at home in a Pirates uniform.

Playing Hurt

Things had gone well for both Roberto and his team in 1956. Yet the new season brought renewed frustration. Roberto suffered from several injuries and he missed forty-three games that summer. His back problem caused him so much pain that he tried playing with a back brace. In July, he even considered quitting baseball for good. "No one knows what it is," Roberto said of his injury, speaking to the United Press. "I run, I throw, I move, it hurts. It goes away and comes back. Someday it hurt, someday no. If it doesn't cure, I quit baseball." Roberto also hurt his throwing arm early in the season while making a sidearm throw during a game. His elbow bothered him a lot and he became very careful with his throwing. He only unleashed the Clemente "cannon" when absolutely necessary.

All in all, 1957 was a forgettable season for Roberto. He finished the year with a .253 batting average. It would be the lowest of his career. The Pirates didn't do any better. They tied for last place in the National League standings.

Many coaches, players, and sportswriters didn't always believe Roberto's claims of injuries. They didn't understand how he could play so well if he was in such terrible pain. Pirates' management also wondered whether Roberto's pain was real. They had his back X-rayed by specialists. The results were inconclusive, as they often are with back and neck injuries. By the end of the 1957 season, Roberto had lost all patience with his nagging back injury. He made it clear that he would not continue to play if he couldn't raise the level of his game. He expected better of himself. He felt the team deserved better.

Roberto had second thoughts about retiring in 1958. His back still bothered him, but he did all he could to manage the pain. Every time he stepped up to the plate, he would roll his shoulders and his head in an effort to loosen the muscles in his back. This ritual continued throughout his career. He appeared in 140 games in the new season and put up better hitting numbers than in 1957. But he fell short of repeating his impressive performance of 1956.

National League president Warren Giles poses with Roberto Clemente in 1965.
Clemente would win a total of four National League batting championships.

During the off-season of 1958–1959, Roberto spent six months with the U.S. Marine Corps. The rigorous conditioning program of the Marines worked wonders on Roberto's back. He began the 1959 season feeling better than he had in years and his playing showed this. During the first two months of the season, Roberto led the team in nearly every hitting category. His Pirate teammates responded to his fine play, and the wins began to pile up. Hopeful Pirates fans began to think that this would be the year that their team would capture the pennant after so many years of failure.

Roberto hurt his elbow in June. He sat on the bench for thirty days. When he rejoined his teammates on the field, his bat had gone cold. His team's hopes for a National League pennant faded quickly. Both Roberto Clemente and the Pittsburgh Pirates were a year away from a breakthrough season.

Roberto started the 1960 season very well. He was impressive during the month of May, hitting .336 with 39 hits and 25 RBIs in 27 games. Baseball writers and broadcasters voted Roberto the National League player of the month. After five years of hard work on the field, he was getting the respect he felt he deserved. Never had Roberto's talents in the field been questioned. Now that his hitting had become steadier, he was coming to be known as a great all-around player.

Clemente opened the season with a three-for-four performance at the plate with two doubles and a single. His average never once dipped below .300 and he ended the season at .314, a career-best so far. Roberto hit 16 home runs and drove in 94 runs, more than he had in any prior season. His RBI total was tops among all Pirates players that summer.

The First World Series

More important for the team, Pittsburgh posted their best record in more than thirty years. They won the National League pennant and went to the World Series. The Pirates were matched against the powerful New York Yankees, the American League champions. Few followers of baseball would have bet against the Yankees that October. They appeared unbeatable, with three power hitters: Mickey Mantle, Roger Maris, and Bill "Moose" Skowron. The Pirates had only one player with more than 20 homers that season. That was first baseman Dick Stuart.

What the Pirates lacked in power at the plate, they made up for in skill on the mound. Their pitching roster looked stronger and deeper than the Yankees'. More than a few baseball experts have said over the years that pitching, not hitting, wins ball games.

Pirate pitchers held the Yankee bats in check in Games 1, 4, and 5. In those three losses, the Yankees scored a combined total of 8 runs. But Pirates pitchers gave up 38 runs in Games 2, 3, and 6. Three wins, three losses. The seventh game would decide who would win the World Series.

Played in Pittsburgh's Forbes Field, Game 7 was another slugfest. This time around, it wasn't just the Yankees who scored runs. Through five innings of play, the Pirates held a 4–1 lead. The Yankees broke through with 4 runs in the sixth. They added to their 5–4 lead in the eighth to take a 7–4 advantage.

Clemente is congratulated as he crosses home plate after hitting a three-run homer. His impressive play during the 1960 season helped the Pirates win the World Series that year.

Pittsburgh battled back, however, and they retook the lead by 9–7 in the bottom of the eighth. Then the Yankees tied the game at nine in the top half of the ninth inning. In the bottom of the ninth, the Pirates' second baseman Bill Mazeroski hit Yankees pitcher Ralph Terry's second pitch of the inning over the wall in left-center field to lift the Pirates to victory. The scrappy Pirates had overcome the highly favored Yankee team. They had won the World Series for the first time in thirty-five years!

A Young Man's Mistakes

Much has been said about Roberto's behavior after the Game 7 victory. The Pirates' right fielder dressed quickly in the locker room, congratulated his teammates, and left the stadium. His teammates had just begun their celebration. According to Roberto's account of what happened that night, he felt that the World Series victory belonged to Pirates fans. He wanted to be out among them on the streets of Pittsburgh.

Years later, Bill Nunn told another version of the events that night. Nunn wrote for the *Pittsburgh Courier* at the time. He said he drove Roberto to the airport immediately after the World Series. He said that Roberto had a ticket for Puerto Rico and wanted to go home. Baseball writers criticized Clemente for not joining his teammates in the locker-room celebration. They didn't believe him when he said that he preferred to be with the fans. They thought he had some other, more selfish motive. They questioned his loyalty to the team.

Whichever version of the story is closer to the truth, it's important to remember that Roberto was still a young man in 1960. He had turned twenty-six that year. He was still learning the ways of baseball and the American people. He was still trying to find his role on the Pirates' team.

The 1950s had been a decade of promising beginnings, disappointing finishes, and, finally, great triumph for Roberto and the Pirates. The 1960s would see the flowering of Roberto's talents. He would finally emerge as a superstar.

Exuberant fans rush onto the field to congratulate the Pittsburgh Pirates on their impressive victory over the New York Yankees in the 1960 World Series.

Most Valiant Player

Although the World Series had concluded, there was one piece of unfinished business for the 1960 season. Every year in mid-November, sportswriters made their selections for the American and National Leagues' Most Valuable Players.

Roberto was not considered a serious candidate for the National League MVP in 1960. His .314 batting average was competitive with the best in the league, but Clemente had not led the league in a single hitting category. Roberto must have known in his heart that he had not yet reached the level of the elite in baseball.

MVP Race

On November 17, the league MVPs were announced. In the American League, Yankee

Clemente's fellow slugger, Roger Maris of the New York Yankees *(above)*, won the 1960 MVP title for the American League. Many thought that Clemente should have won the MVP title for the National League, but it went to Dick Groat.

outfielder Roger Maris took the honors. In the National League, it was the Pirates' Dick Groat who won the batting title with a .325 average. Curiously, Groat had sat out nearly the entire month of September because of a broken wrist. One tends to think of an MVP as a player who can carry a team on his shoulders whenever called upon to do so. None of the Pirates had actually played that role in their championship season. It had been a team effort from start to finish.

Clemente was happy for his teammate but unhappy with the MVP voting. He had finished behind seven other players. Two of those players were Pirates. Pittsburgh's third baseman Don Hoak had placed second. Pirate pitcher Vernon Law had finished seventh. Arguably, neither Hoak nor Law had contributed to the Pirates' success any more than Clemente had. In fact, by some measures Hoak had been less of a contributor. Familiar with the contributions of Hoak and Law, Roberto felt that the sportswriters had intentionally overlooked him because of his race and his Puerto Rican heritage. He resolved to make it much harder for them to ignore his playing in the year to come.

From start to finish of the 1961 season, Clemente was a man on a mission. He set out to prove to the fans, his opponents, his teammates, the press, and himself, that he was one of the game's finest. He had shown greatness in 1960. Yet he was not consistent. Roberto stepped up every aspect of his game, and people began to notice. He was chosen to start both all-star games for the first time in his career.

Did You Know?

From 1959 to 1962, the best players of the National and American Leagues competed against each other in two all-star games during the season. The first took place in early July; the second in early August.

In 1961, the Pirates finished a disappointing sixth in the league. The team's managers could not hold Clemente responsible for Pittsburgh's drop in the standings. He played at a new level all season long, putting up the best numbers of his career. In the process, he won a batting crown for his league-leading .351 average. Roberto also had several personal bests for that season: 572 at-bats, 100 runs scored, 201 hits, and 23 home runs. For the third season in four, Clemente had led the league's right fielders in assists. He threw out twenty-seven runners. Roberto was awarded his first Gold Glove in 1961. He would win twelve straight as the best right fielder in the National League.

Roberto did what he had set out to do when the season began. He had played at the

Determined to prove he was among baseball's finest, Clemente achieved a league-leading .351 batting average and won the first of twelve Gold Gloves in 1961.

top of his game all season long. Clemente, however, was not voted the National League's MVP in 1961. He finished fourth in the voting. Roberto had earned something more important. He had established himself as the Pirates' leader and best player. This was a role that he had wanted for a long time. Many things had held him back in years past—his English, his aching back, the prejudice of others. But that was the past. Roberto had set his mind on breaking through obstacles and finding the best in himself. In doing so, he had earned the respect of his coaches and teammates.

Bad Press

Many of Roberto's frustrations over the years were linked to the way reporters treated him. Looking back, it is clear that the press was not always fair when it reported about Clemente. His complaints about his injuries, however, frequently annoyed reporters. Clemente's expressions of self-confidence had a similar effect. Once, a reporter likened Clemente's play to that of Willie Mays. Instead of thanking the reporter and complimenting Mays, Roberto responded that he didn't play like Willie Mays at all, he played like Roberto Clemente. To the press, the comment sounded both arrogant and disrespectful.

Some of the misunderstandings between Roberto and the press were clearly the result of cultural differences. In the early years of Clemente's career, reporters simply did not have a lot of experience dealing with Hispanic players. Reporters often used American nicknames in place of Roberto's first name. They called him Bob, Bobby, and Robby. This is a good example of the cultural thoughtlessness of the baseball community toward Hispanic players at the time. Was this part of an effort to Americanize Clemente? It seemed that way to him. Roberto never liked the American nicknames that were given to him. Incredibly, they were even used on his baseball cards. He waited until 1969 to see his name appear on his card the way he wanted it to.

New Beginnings

The 1962 season wasn't very memorable for either the Pirates or Clemente. Pirates fans may remember it as the year the team made a late season addition to their roster. They signed outfielder Wilber Stargell. Willie, as he was called, became the regular left fielder in 1963.

Stargell watched Clemente's hard work. He admired Clemente's dedication to the team and his determination to perfect his game. In an interview with writer Bruce Markusen for his book *Roberto Clemente: The Great One*, Stargell explained some of the drills Roberto put himself through to maintain his expert throwing from right field. According to Stargell, Roberto would put a garbage can at third base with the open end facing right field. Then he would ask a teammate or coach to hit balls to him in right field. Roberto practiced fielding the balls and making the throw into the can on one hop. "Tough to do," Stargell told Markusen, "but that's what made him shine a little brighter, stand a little taller." And to this day he still stands taller as the holder of the record for leading the league in outfield assists for five seasons.

The Sly Fox

During games, Clemente tried to lure base runners into taking chances so that he could gun them down. More than a few times he pretended to have trouble fielding a routine hit to right field. If the runner rounded first a little farther than usual with an eye on second base, Roberto would pounce on the ball and rifle it to first base for the tag, sending the surprised runner back to the dugout.

Roberto played well in 1962 and 1963. But both years were a notch below the great level of his play in 1961. The Pirates had settled back in at the bottom of the National League once again, finishing eighth out of the ten teams that made up the league.

Time Off for Love

Roberto returned to Puerto Rico for the winter after every season. One evening in January 1964, he went to the pharmacy to pick up some medication. One of his former teachers, María Isabela Cáceres, worked there. While Roberto was chatting with Ms. Cáceres, a pretty young woman walked in. Roberto wanted to know who she was. Ms. Cáceres told Roberto that her name was Vera Zabala. She worked as a secretary at the Government Development Bank.

Roberto called Vera a few days later at her office and invited her to lunch. But Vera had

Roberto Clemente married Vera Cristina Zabala on November 14, 1964, in his native town of Carolina, Puerto Rico.

been raised to respect Puerto Rican traditions. It would not have been proper for her to accept Roberto's invitation and she told him so. Friends of the two arranged a more appropriate first meeting at a small party. After that, Roberto and Vera had their first date—with chaperones, of course. For the date, Roberto invited Vera to see him play baseball. As luck would have it, it began to rain before Roberto took the field. The game was postponed. After that night, the couple began to see more and more of each other. On November 14, 1964, they were married in their hometown of Carolina, less than a year after they first met.

In between Roberto and Vera's first meeting and their wedding, there was a baseball season to be played. With a sixth-place finish, it was another forgettable one for the Pirates. But Roberto won his second batting crown with a .339 average and he led the league with 211 hits. This was the most he would hit in a single season his entire career. He also hit 40 doubles, a personal-best. But his less-than-spectacular power numbers—12 home runs and 87 RBIs—hurt him in the MVP voting at season's end. Clemente finished a disappointing ninth on sportswriters' ballots.

Racism in America

Every spring, Pirates players faced the humiliation of segregation during training camp in Florida. When the team bus stopped at a restaurant, the black players remained on the bus while the white players ate in the restaurant. This was repeated time and time again throughout the preseason. Roberto and other players became more vocal in protesting this and other injustices. Pirates general manager Joe Brown began to look for ways to help his players preserve their dignity during their time in Florida. Brown had the black players use separate cars. This allowed them to stop at places where they knew they would be served.

Hotels caused a similar problem in the segregated South. During Clemente's first years as a Pirate, the white players stayed at a downtown hotel. The handful of black players stayed in the private home of a prominent African American citizen in Fort Myers. As the number of players of color on the team increased, there were soon too many players for even a large private home. So the Pirates eventually bought a motel that could house everyone on the team.

Improvements in the way the black players were treated did not come quickly enough as far as Roberto was concerned. He would not be satisfied until all players were treated equally. It was during the mid-1960s that Roberto came to know Martin Luther King Jr. Clemente believed in the work of Reverend King. He wanted to do his part to bring about change in baseball.

Race relations were not the only issue that Roberto felt strongly about. As far back as 1959, he had spoken about creating a sports center in Puerto Rico, where all children would be welcome. During the off-season of 1964–1965, Roberto took the first steps towards that dream when he organized and hosted several baseball clinics for underprivileged kids in Puerto Rico.

Bad Luck Season

The new year started badly for Clemente. He experienced the first stroke of bad luck while he was mowing his lawn. The blade of the lawn mower caught hold of a rock and hurled it at Roberto's upper right thigh. He suffered a nasty bruise, but he didn't bother himself about the injury. A few days later he collapsed on the baseball field. A large blood clot had formed around the injury to his leg. Roberto was rushed to the hospital. Doctors operated to remove the clot. During the surgery they discovered a small tear in Roberto's thigh muscle. The problem wasn't serious. His doctor felt that with a week of hospital rest Roberto would be fine.

Disaster struck a second time that spring. Weeks before the start of training camp, Roberto was hospitalized again. This time he suffered from intense fever, chills, nausea, and delirium. The doctors diagnosed the illness as malaria. After several days of treatment, Roberto's condition began to improve. But the illness had taken its toll on him. Clemente had lost twenty pounds. He would not be ready for the start of spring training. The 1965 season was off to a very shaky start.

When Roberto joined his team in Florida, he had regained half of the weight he had lost, but he was still quite weak. The Pirates' management wisely played Roberto sparingly in the preseason allowing him time to rest and to regain his strength in time for the long summer season.

Roberto's 1965 statistics offer a fair measure of his gifts as a ballplayer and his determination to excel. A slow start followed Clemente's lengthy recovery from malaria. Incredibly, he came roaring back to win his third batting title. He appeared in all but nine of Pittsburgh's games that season. This, as much as any other statistic, demonstrates Clemente's strength in the face of adversity.

One flaw in Roberto's game was his lack of power at the plate. In his first eleven seasons, only once had he hit more than 20 homers. He had never driven in more than 100 runs.

Pirates manager Danny Murtaugh retired for health reasons at the end of the 1965 season. The new manager, Harry Walker, took Roberto aside before the 1966 season and told him that the team needed him to hit for power. He actually set targets for his right fielder: 25 home runs and 115 runs batted in.

In 1966, Clemente wowed everyone when he hit a total of 6 home runs over the walls of Forbes Field *(above)* during a three-week stretch.

Power Hitter

Roberto took Walker's words to heart. He began to hit the ball out of the park. In a fifteen-game stretch from late May to early June, Roberto hit 6 home runs. Each was over the walls of Forbes Field, the largest stadium in baseball at the time.

The pennant race was close that year. The Pirates stayed with the Dodgers and the Giants until the very end. They finished third and three games behind the first-place Dodgers. It was a good season for the Pirates, and a great season for Clemente: 202 hits, 105 runs, 31 doubles, 29 home runs, 119 RBIs, and a batting average of .317. He had surpassed the targets that Walker had set for him at the start of the season. He had also quieted the critics who said he couldn't hit for power.

Clemente edged the Dodgers' pitcher Sandy Koufax to take the National League's Most Valuable Player award in 1966. Roberto had won Gold Gloves and batting titles. He had appeared in several all-star games and owned a World Series ring. And the MVP trophy, which had caused him so much disappointment in previous years, was finally his.

In 1966, despite tragedy in his family, Clemente won the MVP trophy, proving that he was a complete player.

Leading the Way to Glory

There are ups and downs in the life of every person. In November 1966, Roberto lost a second brother to cancer. Melchor and Luisa Clemente had experienced much joy and pride as they followed Roberto's career. They had also known great sorrow during that time. Sadly, in just a few short years, further tragedy lay in store for the Clementes.

In January 1967, Pirates general manager Joe Brown met with Roberto to talk about his contract for the upcoming season. Clemente left their meeting with a $100,000 contract. Only four other players earned salaries at this level: Willie Mays, Hank Aaron, Mickey Mantle, and Frank Robinson.

Roberto proved he was worth every penny by winning his fourth National League batting crown in 1967 with a .357 average. He hit for power again that season, belting 23 home runs and driving in 110 runs.

Brush with Death

Before the start of the 1968 season, Roberto had a brush with death while doing work outside his home. He fell about 100 feet down the steep hill on which his house rested. Incredibly, Roberto did no more than tear a muscle in his right shoulder during the fall. The injury caused Clemente to report late to spring training. He played sparingly during the preseason. His shoulder healed slowly and nagged him all season long. Roberto missed thirty games in 1968. He never found his groove at the plate and hit .291. This was his lowest average in ten years. By late summer Roberto was unhappy about his play that season. He told the Pittsburgh press that if his shoulder did not get better during the winter, he would not return for the new season.

Roberto needed time to heal. He decided not to play in the Puerto Rican Winter League. The long break was just what he needed. His shoulder finally healed. Gone were his threats of early retirement. Roberto returned to Florida for the Pirates' training camp.

On March 14, Roberto dove for a foul ball, jamming his left shoulder into the ground. Later Roberto told the press, "My bad shoulder feels good, and my good shoulder feels bad." For years he had reported every one of his ailments and injuries a little too seriously. Now Roberto found the Pittsburgh press much more responsive to his lighthearted way of describing his injuries.

Despite the joke, Roberto's latest injury was serious enough for him to miss most of the preseason. He suited up for opening day, but he continued to have trouble swinging the bat. On April 13, Pittsburgh fans booed their right fielder when he came to the plate in the eighth inning. Roberto tipped his hat to the crowd, and the boos turned to cheers. After the game, Roberto acknowledged that he had not played well. He felt that the fans were right to boo him. We must wonder how any booing could be justified toward a player who had given as much to Pittsburgh and its fans as Roberto had.

Eventually, his injury healed and Clemente's hitting stroke returned. He finished the season with a .345 average and led the league with twelve triples. The Pirates, however, placed third in the National League. Roberto and his teammates had played well, but not well enough to reach the playoffs.

A New Ballpark

After sixty-one years and two World Series championships in the historic Forbes Field, the Pirates moved into a new home. Three Rivers Stadium opened for the second half of the 1970 season. A week later, as part of the festivities linked to the opening of the new park, the Pirates celebrated Roberto Clemente Night. Clemente's parents came to Pittsburgh for the event. This was the first airplane trip ever for ninety-year-old Melchor Clemente. Also standing beside Roberto on the infield of the new stadium were his wife and three sons, Roberto Jr., Enrique, and Luis. More than 43,000 fans came to the game that night and thousands more watched on television via satellite back home in Puerto Rico.

In the days leading up to the event, Clemente had suggested that fans show their support by donating money to Pittsburgh's Children's Hospital. That night, a check for more than $5,000 was given to the hospital on behalf of Clemente and Pirates fans. After the presentation of many gifts and awards, Roberto and his team celebrated on the field with an 11–0 victory over the Houston Astros.

The Pirates had played well during the first half of the season at Forbes Field. They continued to play well in Three Rivers Stadium during the second half. They ended the season tied with the New York Mets at the top of the National League East Division. The teams played a one-game tiebreaker. The Pirates won 2–1. Pittsburgh was now set to host the Cincinnati Reds in the first two

Three Rivers Stadium *(above)* in Pittsburgh, Pennsylvania, opened in 1970
with a gala event celebrating Roberto Clemente's contributions to the Pirates.

games of the National League Championship Series. It had been a hard season for Roberto. He had missed fifty-eight starts, the most of his career. When he did play, he played like the Roberto Clemente of old. But the season had taken its toll on both Clemente and the Pirates. They had very little energy left by the time the hungry Reds came to town. The Pirates lost three straight and were eliminated from the playoffs. Their season was over.

The Mighty Pirates

During the off-season, Joe Brown made several trades to strengthen the Pirates' lineup. His moves paid off. By mid-season 1971, the Pirates were in first place in the National League East. Team chemistry had never been better. Players joked with each other—even with Clemente, who had always been too sensitive to tease.

At one point in the season, two life-sized wax figures of Roberto were delivered to the Pirates' offices. One of them would be sent to the Hall of Fame in Cooperstown, New York. The other was intended for the Pittsburgh Hall of

Fame. Hoping to play a joke on the team doctor, several Pirates players and the team trainer placed one of the wax figures on the trainer's table and called the doctor. They claimed Clemente had passed out. As the story goes, the doctor came running into the room. When he saw Clemente stretched stiffly on the table he tried to take his pulse. When he found none at all, he cried out, "My God! He's cold!" At this point the entire clubhouse burst out laughing. Roberto wasn't there at the time, but he had a good laugh when he learned of the prank.

The Pirates made history on September 1 when they fielded the first-ever all-black starting lineup in the major leagues. Roberto, who had experienced so much prejudice and discrimination in the first several years of his sixteen-year career, must have taken special pride in the Pirates' roster that day.

When the 1971 season ended, the Pirates stood on top of the National League East. They met the San Francisco Giants, the West Division champs, in the National League Championship Series. On October 2, the Giants won the opener

5–4 in Candlestick Park. The Pirates bounced right back and took the next three games to win the pennant. After eleven years, the Pirates were going back to the World Series!

1971 World Series

The Pirates faced the American League champion Baltimore Orioles. The Orioles had the best record in the major leagues. The Orioles also had four twenty-game-winning pitchers. Baltimore's powerful offense supported its top-notch pitching staff. The Orioles looked unstoppable and were the clear favorite to win the series.

The Orioles played like the champs in the first two games at Baltimore's Memorial Stadium, winning 5–3 and 11–3. Game 3, played in Pittsburgh's Three Rivers Stadium, belonged to the Pirates. Final score: 5–1.

Game 4 was the first-ever night game in the history of the World Series. Because it took place on a Wednesday, NBC had pushed for an evening broadcast in the hope of getting a larger audience. The strategy worked. Some 61 million

Americans tuned in to watch the closest game yet in the series. The Pirates held on to win 4–3. The series was tied at two games apiece.

Game 5 featured great pitching by Pirate Nellie Briles. He allowed only two hits and gave up no runs in nine innings, for a 3–0 Pirates victory. The teams returned to Baltimore for Game 6. There, the Orioles edged out the Pirates in ten tense innings for a 3–2 win. The series was now even at three apiece.

Game 7 was another nail-biter. Both teams were scoreless until Clemente belted a solo-shot over the wall in left-center field. Then, in the eighth inning, Pittsburgh added a second run to go up 2–0. Baltimore scored once in their half of the inning, but Pirate shortstop Jackie Hernandez made two clutch plays, one to end the eighth, and a second to end the ninth, to preserve the Pirates' lead and seal their victory.

Clemente had hit in every game of the World Series, as he had in 1960. This time, however, he had done more on the field to help the Pirates, inspiring his teammates with several big plays. One of his greatest moments in

Pirates' players celebrate after winning the 1971 World Series against the Baltimore Orioles. Clemente's outstanding performance in the series won him the MVP title.

the series came in Game 3. On a little tap-back to the Baltimore pitcher, which should have been an easy out, Roberto outran the pitcher, safely reaching first base. This play drove in the first run of the game. Feeding off Roberto's energy, the Pirates fought their way back into the series. Clemente's hustle turned the series around for his team.

For everything he had done, Roberto was voted Most Valuable Player of the World Series. For the first time in seventeen years of major league play, Clemente stood in triumph on the national stage. This was perhaps the greatest moment of his career.

Career Milestone

The Pirates dominated the National League East again in 1972. With several games remaining, the Pirates clinched their third straight divisional title. As the season neared its end, there remained one great, unanswered question for Clemente fans: Would Roberto reach his 3,000th hit that summer?

On September 30, 1972, Roberto Clemente became the first Hispanic and eleventh major league baseball player in history to reach 3,000 hits.

Roberto inched his way to the 2,999-hit mark with only a handful of games left to play. In his final home game of the season, Roberto smashed a double to the wall in left-center field, becoming the eleventh player in major league history to reach 3,000 hits. He was the first Hispanic to join this group of the sport's finest hitters. After the game, Roberto dedicated the hit to the Pittsburgh fans, the people of Puerto Rico, and to Roberto Marín, who had launched Roberto's baseball career more than twenty years earlier.

More Pennant Dreams

The Pirates faced the National League West Division champion Cincinnati Reds for the pennant. This was their second meeting in three years. The teams split the first four games. Game 5, the final game of the series, wasn't decided until the last inning when the Reds overcame a 3–2 Pirate lead to claim the pennant. Roberto didn't know it at the time, but he had just played his last major league game.

A Final Tragedy

Three months later, on December 23, 1972, a massive earthquake jolted Nicaragua, killing more than 7,000 people and leaving another 250,000 homeless. Roberto had visited this small Central American country only a month earlier. His heart went out to the Nicaraguan people in their time of crisis. When he was asked to become honorary chairman of the Puerto Rican earthquake relief committee, he accepted immediately.

Roberto worked fourteen-hour days on Christmas Eve, Christmas Day, and the day after. He asked for donations of food, clothing, and other supplies from the citizens of Puerto Rico. He helped fill the relief packages for delivery. In all, the committee raised $150,000 and collected twenty-six tons of food, clothing, and medicine. Three flights were made to transport the goods to Managua, the capital of the devastated country. Just before New Year's Day, a fourth flight was arranged to assist with additional donations that had come in. Roberto

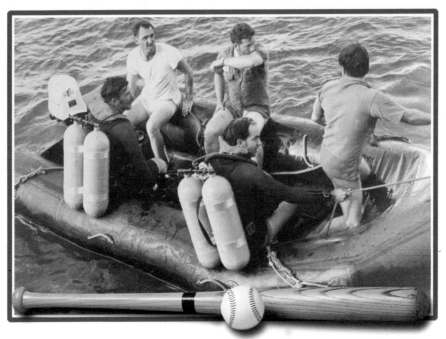

Divers desperately searched for the bodies of Roberto Clemente and others following the fatal crash of the plane bound for Nicaragua to deliver aid.

learned that some of the deliveries weren't reaching the people of Nicaragua. Apparently, the army was taking charge of the goods. Roberto volunteered to travel with the fourth transport flight in hopes of intervening on behalf of the people.

The plane carrying Clemente, four other men, and eight tons of supplies was in sad shape. It was overloaded by more than two tons. The aircraft also suffered from mechanical problems. Roberto was unaware of these details.

After several delays on the ground, the plane was finally cleared for takeoff from San Juan International Airport, nineteen hours after its scheduled departure. Shortly after it left the ground, the plane appeared to be in trouble. The pilot seemed to be trying to return to the airport. Then there was an explosion, followed by three more. The plane burst into flames and headed directly toward the ocean. Seconds later, it had disappeared under water.

Rescue parties, joined by the U.S. Coast Guard and Navy, searched and searched. Little of the plane could be found. After several hours, a pair of glasses was discovered. Later, a briefcase and life jackets were found. Several days later, the pilot's body was recovered. No traces of the other four men were ever discovered.

Grieving Fans and Memorials

The people of Puerto Rico and Pittsburgh, and baseball fans everywhere mourned the death of one of the game's best. The world had lost more than a fine athlete. Gone too, was a great human being.

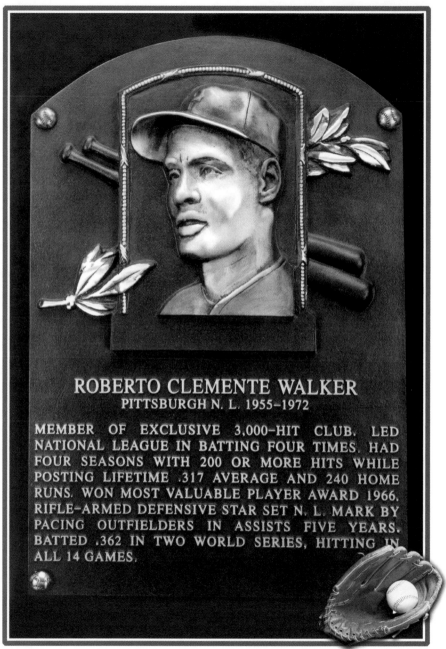

ROBERTO CLEMENTE WALKER
PITTSBURGH N. L. 1955-1972

MEMBER OF EXCLUSIVE 3,000-HIT CLUB. LED
NATIONAL LEAGUE IN BATTING FOUR TIMES. HAD
FOUR SEASONS WITH 200 OR MORE HITS WHILE
POSTING LIFETIME .317 AVERAGE AND 240 HOME
RUNS. WON MOST VALUABLE PLAYER AWARD 1966.
RIFLE-ARMED DEFENSIVE STAR SET N. L. MARK BY
PACING OUTFIELDERS IN ASSISTS FIVE YEARS.
BATTED .362 IN TWO WORLD SERIES, HITTING IN
ALL 14 GAMES.

Like most people of Spanish heritage, Clemente carried both his father's (Clemente) and his mother's (Walker) last names. When it inducted Clemente in 1973, the Baseball Hall of Fame mistakenly wrote his name as Roberto Walker Clemente. In 2000, the Hall of Fame corrected the mistake with a plaque that reads "Roberto Clemente Walker."

A few years before his death, Roberto had begun a project that gained momentum in the years after his passing. His dream of a *ciudad deportiva*, a sports city where all Puerto Rican children would be welcome, became a reality.

The Puerto Rican government donated 233 acres of land in 1973. After ten years of fund-raising, construction of the sports complex began. Today, the center contains four regulation baseball fields, two softball fields, one Little League field, three basketball courts, four tennis courts, four volleyball courts, and an Olympic-size swimming pool, as well as many, many children on any given day.

Clemente's dream of helping the children of Puerto Rico comes true every day at Roberto Clemente's Sports City. Vera Clemente and her sons continue to be involved with the institution. Their goal is to teach children to play sports as well as become kind, caring citizens of the world. Roberto would have been proud.

ROBERTO CLEMENTE *TIMELINE*

⚾	**Aug. 18 1934**	Roberto Clemente Walker is born in Carolina, Puerto Rico.
⚾	**Nov. 1952**	Signs first professional contract with the Santurce Cangrejeros of the Puerto Rican Winter League.
⚾	**Feb. 19 1954**	Signs one-year contract with the Brooklyn Dodgers.
⚾	**Nov. 22 1954**	Is selected first in the draft by the Pittsburgh Pirates.
⚾	**Apr. 17 1955**	Plays in first major league game.
⚾	**May 1960**	Is voted National League Player of the Month.
⚾	**Oct. 1960**	Pittsburgh Pirates defeat New York Yankees in World Series.
⚾	**Nov. 1961**	Wins first of twelve straight Gold Gloves as the National League's premier defensive right fielder.
⚾	**Nov. 14 1961**	Marries Vera Cristina Zabala in Carolina, Puerto Rico.
⚾	**Nov. 1966**	Is selected the National League's Most Valuable Player.

	Jan. 25 **1967**	Signs one-year contract for $100,000, the highest single-season salary in Pirates history at the time.
	July 24 **1970**	The city of Pittsburgh celebrates Roberto Clemente Night at recently opened Three Rivers Stadium.
	Sept. 1 **1971**	The Pittsburgh Pirates become the first team to field an all-black starting lineup in a major league game.
	Oct. **1971**	Pittsburgh Pirates defeat Baltimore Orioles in World Series; Clemente named series MVP.
	Sept. 30 **1972**	Records 3,000th and final hit of his career.
	Dec. 31 **1972**	Dies in plane crash while attempting to transport supplies to earthquake victims in Nicaragua.
	Aug. 6 **1973**	Is inducted into the National Baseball Hall of Fame.

Glossary

adversity Difficult or trying times.

arrogant Unpleasantly proud.

chaperone An older person who goes along on a young couple's date to make sure they behave properly.

clean-up hitter The fourth batter in a team's lineup.

confide To share a secret or information with another person.

consistent Performing at the same level over a period of time.

delirium Temporary mental disorder, often triggered by severe fever, during which the patient can't tell the real from the imaginary.

destined Chosen (as if by fate) to be or do something.

diamond Baseball field.

dismay Feeling a mixture of disappointment and surprise.

draft To choose new players from a pool of talented prospects.

emerge To come out.

idol A person admired and looked up to by others.

inconclusive Not sufficient to decide or settle a question.

ineffective Not producing good results.

ineligible Not meeting the requirements to participate or to compete in an event.

intervene To come between people or groups who do not agree or are in conflict.

isolated To be alone; separated from other people.

negotiate To deal or bargain with another person.

pennant   In baseball, the flag that represents a league championship; the championship itself.

(pitching) rotation   A team's starting pitchers and the order in which they appear in games.

plantation   A large farm, usually in a tropical area.

potential   Possibilities within a person.

preserve   To keep alive or safe; protect.

prominent   Important and well-known.

resolve   To set one's mind to something.

roster   List of players on a team.

sacrifice   To do without something for the benefit of another.

tragic   Dreadful; disastrous; fatal.

triple-A   Highest class of minor league baseball, followed by double-A and single-A.

For More Information

The National Baseball Hall of Fame
   and Museum
25 Main Street
P.O. Box 590
Cooperstown, NY 13326
(888) 425-5633
Web site: http://www.baseballhalloffame.org

The Pittsburgh Pirates
PNC Park
115 Federal Street
Pittsburgh, PA 15212
(412) 323-5000
Web site:
   http://pirates.mlb.com/nasapp/mlb/pit/
   homepage/pit_homepage.jsp

The Roberto Clemente Foundation
320 East North Avenue
Pittsburgh, PA 15212
(412) 231-2300
Web site:
 http://www.robertoclementefoundation.org

Web Sites

Due to the changing nature of Internet links, the Rosen Publishing Group, Inc., has developed an online list of Web sites related to the subject of this book. This site is updated regularly. Please use this link to access the list:

http://www.rosenlinks.com/bbhf/rocl/

For Further Reading

Bjarkman, Peter. *Baseball Legends: Roberto Clemente*. New York: Chelsea House, 1991.

Dunham, Montrew. *Childhoods of Famous Americans: Roberto Clemente, Young Ball Player*. New York: Simon and Schuster, 1997.

Engel, Trudie. *We'll Never Forget You, Roberto Clemente*. New York: Scholastic, 1996.

Hano, Arnold. *Roberto Clemente, Batting King*. New York: Putnam, 1968.

Macht, Norman. *A Junior Hispanics Achievement Book: Roberto Clemente*. New York: Chelsea House, 1994.

Markusen, Bruce. *Roberto Clemente: The Great One*. Champaign, IL: Sports Publishing, Inc., 1998.

Wagenheim, Kal, and Wilfred Sheed. *Clemente!* Chicago: Olmstead Press, 2001.

Bibliography

Bjarkman, Peter. *Baseball with a Latin Beat*. Jefferson, NC: McFarland, 1994.

Christine, Bill. *Numero Uno: Roberto*. New York: Stadia Sports, 1973.

Hano, Arnold. *Roberto Clemente, Batting King*. New York: Putnam, 1968.

Markusen, Bruce. *Roberto Clemente: The Great One*. Champaign, IL: Sports Publishing, 1998.

Musick, Phil. *Who Was Roberto?* Garden City, NY: Doubleday, 1974.

O'Brien, Jim. *Remember Roberto.*
Pittsburgh, PA: Jim O'Brien
Publishing, 1994.

Wagenheim, Kal. *Clemente*. New York:
Praeger, 1973.

Index

About the Author

Robert Kingsbury is an editor of foreign language learning materials. He lives in Philadelphia, Pennsylvania, with his wife and two daughters. Since 1984, he has had a Roberto Clemente stamp in his wallet. This is Robert's second book.

Photo Credits

Cover, pp. 58, 60, 68, 88 © AP/Wide World Photos; p. 5 © The Topps Company, Inc.; pp. 6, 10, 13, 23, 27, 30, 34, 43, 46, 50, 54–55, 74, 76, 94 © Bettman/Corbis; p. 8 © Steve Dunwell/Image Bank; pp. 15, 38–39, 90–91 © National Baseball Hall of Fame Library, Cooperstown, N.Y.; p. 63 © Rusty Kennedy/AP/Wide World Photos; pp. 82–83 © Dave Arrigo/AP/Wide World Photos; p. 96 © Will Waldron/AP/Wide World Photos. Baseball Graphics: Corbis Royalty Free.

Roberto Clemente

Editor
Mark Beyer

Series Design and Layout
Geri Giordano